# Bearded Dragons : A Guide From A Veterinarian On Caring For Your Bearded Dragon

## Make Your Dragon Live For 12 Years Or More

By: Donald Wilson

ISBN-13: 978-1478135845

# Publishers Notes

## BINDERS PUBLISHING LLC

Disclaimer

This publication is intended to provide helpful and informative material. It is not intended to diagnose, treat, cure, or prevent any health problem or condition, nor is intended to replace the advice of a physician. No action should be taken solely on the contents of this book. Always consult your physician or qualified health-care professional on any matters regarding your health and before adopting any suggestions in this book or drawing inferences from it.

The author and publisher specifically disclaim all responsibility for any liability, loss or risk, personal or otherwise, which is incurred as a consequence, directly or indirectly, from the use or application of any contents of this book.

Any and all product names referenced within this book are the trademarks of their respective owners. None of these owners have sponsored, authorized, endorsed, or approved this book.

Always read all information provided by the manufacturers' product labels before using their products. The author and publisher are not responsible for claims made by manufacturers.

The statements made in this book have not been evaluated by the Food and Drug Administration.

Binders Publishing LLC
7950 NW 53rd Street
Miami,
FL 33166

Donald Wilson

Kindle Edition 2012

BINDERS PUBLISHING PRESS is a trademark of Binders Publishing LLC.

For information about special discounts for bulk purchases, please contact Binders Publishing Sales Department at 646-312-7900 or publishing@binderspublishing.com

Designed by Colin WF Scott

Manufactured in the United States of America


ISBN-13: 978-1478135845

Donald Wilson

# Table of Contents

CHAPTER 1- WHAT YOU NEED TO KNOW ABOUT DRAGONS BEFORE YOU BUY THEM ..................................................................7

CHAPTER 2- HOW TO TELL THE GENDER OF A DRAGON ...................9

CHAPTER 3- DIFFERENT SPECIES OF DRAGONS AND WHICH ONE MAKES THE BEST PET ..............................................................................10

CHAPTER 4- CREATING THE RIGHT ENVIRONMENT FOR YOUR DRAGON'S LAIR : PROVIDING A GOOD HABITAT ...............................12

CHAPTER 5- WHAT TO FEED YOUR BEARDED DRAGON TO MAKE HIM LIVE LONGER : THE BEST FOOD AND SCHEDULES TO FEED YOUR PET....................................................................................................14

CHAPTER 6- HOW TO MONITOR THE HEALTH OF YOUR DRAGON : COMMON HEALTH ISSUES AND HOW TO TREAT THEM ...................16

CHAPTER 7- WHICH OTHER PETS TO PUT IN WITH YOUR DRAGON ..................................................................................................................18

CHAPTER 8- BREEDING YOUR DRAGONS : HOW TO FIND THE RIGHT MATE AND THE PROCESS .............................................................20

CHAPTER 9- TIPS FOR PET DRAGON OWNERS.....................................22

ABOUT THE AUTHOR .................................................................................24

# Dedication

I want to dedicate this book to Angela, my dragon at home, she is are great friends with my tortoise and loves to follow him around. It is her good nature that makes me want to tell people how to care for their bearded dragon.

# CHAPTER 1- WHAT YOU NEED TO KNOW ABOUT DRAGONS BEFORE YOU BUY THEM

Beared dragons belong to a group of diurnal lizards that belong to the Agamidae family. They are mostly small or middle-sized and are calm, quiet creatures. Captive bearded dragons make very good pets, who are very easy to breed.

Before you take the step to purchase a bearded dragon as a pet, it is very necessary for you to make an assessment of your lifestyle to see if he will fit comfortably in it, and if you will have the time that it will take to take care of this animal. They like to be touched and held so this is not an animal that you will not need to have much interaction with except for feeding it and cleaning its habitat like you can do with other animals.

You will need to have a flat surface that can accommodate a tank that is at least between twenty and forty gallons. In addition, if you do have other animals in the home, you will need to ensure that they will not be able to attack him. You should also have enough time at least one time each week to properly clean his tank which involves removing both droppings and food that has gone uneaten.

Your assessment as to whether or not you should get a bearded dragon would also include your finances, as it will cost you to maintain and care for this animal. There is of course food, but there is also the cost for setting up the tank to make it perfect for him, plus you will have to change the light bulbs every six months and take him to the vet every year to check for parasites.

# Chapter 2- How To Tell The Gender Of A Dragon

It is not very difficult to find out the gender of your bearded dragon. To do so, you simply need to place the dragons on their back in a laying position in your palm securing it properly and then softly pull its tail back. If you see two lumps above its leg then it is a male. The female bearded dragon is smaller and their heads are narrower and pointier than the males. The males have femoral pores that are larger than the females, which can be found on the base of their thighs. You will have to wait until they are a few months old to be able to tell their sex though.

Bearded dragons find it difficult to breathe when they are on their backs, so if you are having a difficulty determining its sex and it is taking longer than usual, you should turn them over on their stomach and simply turn their tail to face you. You should then very tenderly place your thumb on their back and then gently lift his tail. If you to the check too soon you may see just one bump on the male and mistake it for a female. Additionally, the tails of the males tend to be thicker and the beards of the males are sometimes blacker than the females as well.

Yet another means of determining the gender of a bearded dragon is called probing. However, this is not recommended for anyone other than the veterinarian to do. This method involves exposing the sex glands via the vent and can be very harmful to the animal if it is not properly done by an expert.

# CHAPTER 3- DIFFERENT SPECIES OF DRAGONS AND WHICH ONE MAKES THE BEST PET

You can find many different kinds of bearded dragons that are sold as pets, any either pet stores or at pet shows. The different species will have different coloring, appearance, sizes and even differ in their temperament as well.

Among the species of bearded dragons that make the best pets include the Inland bearded dragon, the Coastal bearded dragon and the Rankin bearded dragon. The Inland bearded dragon is also known as the Central bearded dragon, they are usually brown or tan in color. This species is a native of Australia and usually can be found in the mainland but they will also be seen occasionally near the coastal areas in the east and south of Australia as well. This species does very well in captivity and they do breed very well. They are very popular as pets, and as such, you can get them at a very affordable cost. The Inland bearded dragons can be identified by the two unique spots that are on the base of their necks.

The Coastal bearded dragons are common to both the south and the east of Australia. They are about the same size as the Inland bearded dragons but their coloring is darker. They are a little more aggressive than the Inland bearded dragon, and are also stronger and can better tolerate high humidity and cold weather.

The Rankin bearded dragon is usually found close the central as well as the west of Australia. They are quite small; about thirteen inches in length and the do not have an inflatable beard.

Bearded dragons make great pets because of their very docile nature and they do not bite. They are also easy to feed and they are very responsive to the human voice. They loved to be touched and held and they love to have their heads rubbed. They have a greeting behavior wherein they lift their front legs in a motion that is almost circular so that it seems as if they are actually waving. Bearded dragons usually live to be about ten years old, but have also been known to live longer as well.

# CHAPTER 4- CREATING THE RIGHT ENVIRONMENT FOR YOUR DRAGON'S LAIR : PROVIDING A GOOD HABITAT

To keep your bearded dragon happy and healthy you will have to create the perfect environment for them to live in captivity. If you are housing them in an aquarium it has to have a lid that is tightly fitted. The baby bearded dragons should be kept in an aquarium that is at least ten to fifteen gallons, while the adults should be housed in an aquarium that is at least fifty five to sixty gallons.

Wire cages are not usually recommended as a habitat for bearded dragons as they can cause trauma to their nose and foot and they do not retain heat. However, if you decide to use a wire cage you will need to ensure that the wire is coated plastic to reduce the possibility of injuries.

The design of your cages should easily facilitate its careful cleaning. If it is a wood cage it should be sealed with polyurethane or another agent that waterproofs the cage. The joints should also be caulked. The substrate that is used to line the cage should be digestible if swallowed by the bearded dragon, absorbent and clean. It can be made of flat newspaper, rolls of brown paper, Astro Turf or indoor or outdoor carpet. Cedar shavings, kitty litter, corn on the cob that has been crushed or potting soil that has in pesticides, fertilizer, wetting agents or vermiculite should never be used.

Their habitat should also have branches so that they can climb and bask on them. These branches should be secured, of different sizes and have no sap or pitch. Oak branches are usually a very good choice. The branches should be as wide as the bearded dragon to avoid him being injured by it. You can also place smooth rocks in their habitat as well as this will help the wear down their toenails that should be clipped often when they are in captivity. A hiding place would also be welcomed by the bearded dragon so you could place a cardboard tube, an empty cardboard box or a flower pot in their cage.

Their habitat should also be properly heated as they are cold-blooded creatures. To ensure that they are getting the required temperature, you need t ensure that their habitat is at between 78-88 Fahrenheit in the day time and somewhere in the 70s during the nights. Two thermometers should be placed inside their housing; one at the level where they bask and the other closer to the floor to ensure that they are also getting the required temperature. Their primary light source in captivity should come from incandescent lights placed over their cage. These lights should be turned off at nights and depending on the temperature surrounding the cage, you may need a secondary heat source. This can be provided by either a heating pad that should be placed under the cage or via nocturnal incandescent light bulbs.

Different types of lights are crucial to the health of the bearded dragon. Incandescent bulbs provide them with both heat and visible white light. You can use a mixture of fluorescent and incandescent light fixtures to give them visible light. They will also need natural sunlight so to maintain their good health you will have to ensure that they are getting a certain degree of ultraviolet light referred to as UVB as they need this in order to produce vitamin D. If you are unable to provide them with natural sunlight, then a special light that provides the UVB light should be used.

Your bearded dragon's cage and his food and water bowls should be properly cleaned at least once a week using a mixture that is ten parts water and one part household bleach. They should be left to dry completely. Your hand should always be washed both before and after you handle the dragon to avoid the spread of salmonella. You may want to invest in some rubber gloves to use when you are cleaning their habitat.

# CHAPTER 5- WHAT TO FEED YOUR BEARDED DRAGON TO MAKE HIM LIVE LONGER : THE BEST FOOD AND SCHEDULES TO FEED YOUR PET

A balanced diet is very vital to the health and survival of your bearded dragon. They are ravenous creatures who need to be fed a number of times a day, but their diets will be different depending on their age. Bearded dragons are actually omnivorous creatures, which mean that they eat vegetables, fruits and insects. They should be fed something from the vegetable, fruits and insects food groups at each feeding. Your baby bearded dragon will need more protein in their diet to help with their growing tissues and bones but they also need their vegetables.

The live insects that your bearded dragon usually eats are crickets (which is their favorite), Dubia roaches, superworms and waxworms, among others. The crickets should always be gut loaded the night before feeding them to the dragons. The foods you feed them should be proportionate to the bearded dragon as foods that are too big for them to digest can cause seizures, blockages in their intestines as well as malnutrition.

Your bearded dragons that are between the ages of hatchlings to six months old should be fed fifty crickets each day, which should be split into two to three smaller feedings. Bearded dragons that are 6 to 9 months old should get thirty crickets every day. When they are between 9 and 12 months they can be given thirty crickets every other day. When they get to a year old they can be given fifty crickets per week, fed either every day or every other day.

# Chapter 6- How To Monitor The Health Of Your Dragon : Common Health Issues And How To Treat Them

Bearded dragons usually have very good health and will remain healthy while in captivity once their owners pay attention to their heath needs. There is a list of illnesses that are common to bearded dragon however. These are genetic diseases, calcium and vitamin D3 deficiencies, Beta-Carotine deficiencies, and illnesses related to overfeed and the injuries they get when they show aggressive behaviors. They also suffer from respiratory infections, gastrointestinal infections, fungal infections and egg binding.

The genetic diseases that the bearded dragons are prone to include extra appendages as well as deformed tails and limbs. If they are deficient in calcium and vitamin D3 they may have stunted growth, poor bone growth, brittle bones and seizures. You can avoid and cure these deficiencies by ensuring that they get proper dietary supplements and lighting. When they are deficient in Beta-Carotine, this will cause their color to fade over time. To avoid and cure this deficiency you should include yellow vegetables and carrots in their diet.

When a bearded dragon is overfed as babies this can cause their hind quarters to become paralyzed and they usually end up dead. Too much food or foods that are too large will put too much pressure on their food bolus on their spinal cord paralyzing and then eventually killing them.

16

Bearded dragons that are housed together often times cause injuries to each other, and the less aggressive ones are the ones that usually sustain the more serious injuries. This may cause them to lose toes or the tips of their tails. These injuries must not be left untreated, but should be treated with a disinfectant ointment. You should put them in separate cages if the fighting persists.

Their respiratory infections will be manifested in their noisy breathing, gaping as well as a mucus discharge from their mouth and their nose. This is usually caused by high humidity or low temperatures or both. They should be kept in fairly low humidity and should also be taken to a Herp veterinarian.

When your bearded dragon has a gastrointestinal infection they will lose weight, have no appetite, have diarrhea and have a foul smell. They should be immediately taken to the veterinarian to be treated for this as well. A warm, damp environment is usually the cause for fungal infections in a bearded dragon. It presents as a scrape or a cut on the animal and can be treated with an anti-fungal cream.

Calcium deficiency can cause egg binding in your bearded dragon. If they are either underweight or overweight or are unable to locate a suitable egg nest, then this can also cause egg binding. If the latter is the cause for the egg binding, then you should provide him with a soil substrate that is deep so they can dig their nest. However, if it is caused by any other reason, then they must be taken to the veterinarian.

# CHAPTER 7- WHICH OTHER PETS TO PUT IN WITH YOUR DRAGON

There are really no other animals that I could think of recommending to be housed in the same cage as a bearded dragon. This is so due to the fact that as a rule, they really seem to prefer to live on their own. If you are thinking of housing two bearded dragons together, the fact is that two male bearded dragons may fight and even kill each other.

As such, this may not be the smartest choice of a housemate for a bearded dragon. Some persons have reported that they have successfully housed two female bearded dragons who have not shown any real form of aggression towards each other. However, there is always the danger of one being a little more dominant than the other and this may result in a lot of stress for the one that is a little less dominant.

In addition, it is advised that you should not put different species of bearded dragons to live together in the same habitat. This is mainly due to the fact that different species require different care with may include different humidity, different food and different temperature. However, some persons have said that they have housed their bearded dragons with a completely different reptile; namely the Uromastyx and they have lived together peaceably and the same temperature and humidity worked quite will for them both. Nevertheless, this is not something that would be recommended on a general or regular basis even though a small number of persons have had no real problems doing this.

The fact is that bearded dragons; even though they are usually very docile creatures who just love to be handled by human beings, they are quite territorial and when it comes to other animals they may cause harm them if they are placed in the same cage.

# CHAPTER 8- BREEDING YOUR DRAGONS : HOW TO FIND THE RIGHT MATE AND THE PROCESS

To breed your bearded dragons you will need to first house them in two different cages, and then introduce them to each other so that they will gradually become accustomed to each other and not aggress when they are placed tougher for mating. The male is then allowed to move in with the female for a short time until mating is over and then the male should be placed back in his own cage.

The female will lay between ten and thirty five eggs and the eggs should be laid in about a month after mating has taken place. She should be provided a sufficient amount of sand for her to dig in, and you can even provide what is referred to as a hiding box for her to lay the eggs in. When the eggs have been laid you should use a spoon to remove them from her cage and any extremely dented or yellows eggs should be discarded.

The eggs should then be kept in an incubator at between twenty eight and thirty one degrees Celsius and at about fifty percent humidity. Vermiculite would be a better substrate for the eggs instead of sand, since sand may impact on the egg. The eggs usually take between sixty and eighty days to hatch. A majority of the eggs will live, while some may be infertile or may die.

It is important to note that you will need to have enough room for the hatchlings even prior to breeding your bearded dragon. A very good habitat for your hatchlings is a Rubbermaid container with the right substrate.

In addition, the male should be watched very closely during the mating season as the male sometimes tend to get very aggressive towards the female. The feces of the female should also be checked by a veterinarian prior to breeding her as well. This will tell you whether or not she is well enough to mate and breed.

# CHAPTER 9- TIPS FOR PET DRAGON OWNERS

Although bearded dragons prefer to live on their own, they love to be cuddled and handled by human beings. Crickets are a favorite treat for most of the bearded dragon species who can live to be ten years or older once they are properly fed and taken care of.

There are many interesting tidbits about these animals. For instance, they communicate with each other by bobbing their heads, sometimes in a show of aggression as well as by hand waves as if to say leave me alone.

Bearded dragons usually go through a phase called brumation, or what is referred to as a winter shutdown, when they are a lot less active and eat a lot less and may hide in different places in the cage. When this happens, their temperature should be lowered to between sixty and seventy degrees and given basking temperatures of between seventy five and eighty five degrees. This period can last for a few weeks or for months. Dragons that are eighteen months old or older will go through brumation on a yearly basis.

They also have what is called a parietal or a third eye on the top of their head. This is usually used in the detection of predators above them. They also have a small flap that covers over their nostrils and this is used to protect their nose from objects such as sand.

If your bearded dragon's beard puffs out or becomes black, this is usually a normal occurrence. The males tend to do this much more often than females, but they both do it as a sign of excitement, when they are spooked or ready to mate. If the beard is constantly black however, this may be a sign of pain or that something needs to be changed in their habitat.

Your bearded dragon should be given fresh water in their bowl every day and the water bowl should be disinfected once away so that there is not a build-up of any kind of bacteria. Some bearded dragons may refuse to drink from a water bowl. As such, you may need to slowly drip water into their snouts.

You should bathe your bearded dragon at least once a week and this will help to keep them hydrated and assist them with the shedding process as well. The water should be warm when it is tested on your wrist, similar to the temperature of the bath water for a little child. The water should be only as deep as the height of the dragon's chest of just half way up to their front arms and they should never be left unattended in the water.

# ABOUT THE AUTHOR

Donald Wilson loves all aquatic animals, but reptiles are his favorite. He however has a special love for turtles and bearded dragons. He grew up as an only child but he never craved another sibling due to the fact that he always had animals around him. He always wanted a turtle or a bearded dragon but his parents decided that they were much too busy to spend the time that was needed to care for these animals, and he was too young at one point, and then way too busy himself with both school and athletics by the time he got to the age where he was old enough to look after one.

As such, it was not until he was out of college and settled in his career that he decided to get not one, but two turtles; a Red eared Slider and a Painted Turtle and one male and one female bearded dragon. He knows all there is to know about turtles and bearded dragons and enjoys sharing his vast knowledge about them with all those who are interested in learning about these creatures just for their general knowledge but also those who are considering them as pets.

He sees his turtles as his lifetime friends as they are among the longest living creatures in existence and although they do take a lot of care, it is completely worth it to him and he loves his friendly little bearded dragons who close their eyes when he rubs their heads.

10955638R00015

Printed in Great Britain
by Amazon.co.uk, Ltd.,
Marston Gate.